Mastering Behaviour Detection:
Security Awareness and Response Strategies

In a world increasingly shaped by complex threats and evolving security risks, understanding and mastering the science of behavior detection is more crucial than ever.

The ability to interpret subtle cues, recognize indicators of potential threats, and respond swiftly can mean the difference between vulnerability and resilience. This book is born from the commitment to bridge knowledge with practice, offering a comprehensive guide for professionals seeking to elevate their security awareness, enhance response capabilities, and foster a proactive culture of vigilance.

Drawing upon both foundational concepts and advanced strategies, Mastering Behaviour Detection explores the intricacies of human behavior as a cornerstone of effective security. Each chapter delves into techniques refined by experts, blending psychological insights with actionable steps to empower readers in the field of security and beyond.

From situational awareness to advanced response tactics, this book aims to transform the way we think about, respond to, and mitigate risks. Whether you are a seasoned professional or new to the field, this book will provide you with the tools to not only detect and understand behavior but also to respond strategically in real time. Together, let's set a new standard in security awareness and preparedness.

Mastering Behaviour Detection: Security, Awareness, and Response Strategies

Table of Contents
Chapter 1: Behaviour Detection Manager (BDM)

Chapter 2: Behaviour Detection Officer (BDO)

Chapter 3: Behaviour Detection Awareness (BDA)

Chapter 4: Threat Image Recognition Training (TIRT) 3D & 2D

- The Role of Technology in Threat Detection
- TIRT: Why It Matters
- 2D vs. 3D Image Recognition
- Case Studies and Real-World Scenarios

Chapter 5: Behaviour Detection Techniques and Application

- Understanding Hostile Reconnaissance
- Key Indicators of Reconnaissance
- Practical Techniques for Detecting Reconnaissance
- Staff Training for Reconnaissance Awareness
- Debriefing and Reporting Processes

Chapter 6: Hostile Reconnaissance and Security Awareness

- Introduction to Behaviour Detection
- Identifying Baselines and Anomalies
- Techniques for Effective Detection
- Legal Framework: Martyn's Law

- Recent Threats and the Role of Behaviour Detection

Chapter 1: Behaviour Detection Manager (BDM)

Introduction to the Role of a BDM: Managing Threats in an Unpredictable World

In today's rapidly evolving global security landscape, the role of the Behaviour Detection Manager (BDM) has become not just essential but absolutely crucial. Threats to organizations—whether stemming from terrorism, organized crime, insider threats, or sophisticated cyber-attacks—have become increasingly complex and nuanced, making early detection not just important, but vital for the safety and integrity of operations. BDMs carry the significant responsibility of overseeing Behaviour Detection Officers (BDOs), seamlessly integrating them into broader security operations, and ensuring that any potential risks are identified, escalated, and addressed as promptly as possible.

The BDM is far more than just a supervisor; they are the pivotal decision-maker who ensures that a range of behaviour detection techniques are applied both efficiently and effectively.

To excel in this role, they must possess a deep understanding of the extensive threat landscape while managing their teams to recognize and address emerging threats in real-time. From overseeing daily operations to making critical decisions during crises, a BDM's responsibilities are multi-layered, intricate, and dynamic.

This chapter delves into the essential components of building a cohesive and effective security strategy through behaviour detection, managing and leading a team of BDOs, and responding decisively to threats. Real-world examples will be used to illustrate best practices and highlight what to do—and what pitfalls to avoid—in critical situations, providing invaluable insights for those in the field.

Understanding the Threat Landscape: From Internal to External Threats

A comprehensive understanding of the threat landscape is critical to any successful security operation. For a BDM, threats can be categorized into two main types: external and internal.

- **External Threats:** These typically involve entities outside of the organization, such as terrorist groups, cybercriminals, or corporate espionage agents. These actors may target the organization with the intent of causing physical or financial harm, stealing information, or disrupting operations.

- **Internal Threats:** These are threats that originate within the organization, often from employees, contractors, or insiders who misuse their access or knowledge. Examples include disgruntled employees seeking revenge, or individuals engaged in corporate espionage.

The BDM must remain vigilant for both types of threats, continuously assessing risks and ensuring that their Behaviour Detection Officers are trained to recognize early signs of each. This requires setting up effective monitoring procedures, implementing a robust training program, and maintaining up-to-date knowledge of the latest threat trends.

The threat landscape encompasses a wide variety of risks that organizations face, ranging from internal to external threats. Understanding this landscape is crucial for developing effective security strategies.

Internal threats originate from within the organization and can be classified into several categories. Insider threats may arise from employees, contractors, or business partners who misuse their access to sensitive information. This can be intentional, such as data theft or sabotage, or unintentional, such as negligence in handling data. Additionally, technological vulnerabilities, such as weak access controls or inadequate security policies, can also lead to breaches from internal sources.

External threats are typically perpetrated by individuals or groups outside the organization. These can include cybercriminals, hacktivists, and nation-state actors. Common external threats include phishing attacks, ransomware, malware, and denial-of-service attacks. These threats often exploit vulnerabilities in systems and can lead to significant financial losses, reputational damage, and legal consequences.

The convergence of internal and external threats creates a complex security environment. For instance, an external attacker may exploit an internal vulnerability, such as employee credentials obtained through phishing. This highlights the need for a holistic approach to security that addresses both internal and external threats.

Organizations must implement robust security measures, including employee training, access controls, regular security audits, and incident response plans. Continuous monitoring and threat intelligence can also help organizations stay ahead of emerging threats and adapt their security posture accordingly.

By understanding the full spectrum of threats, organizations can better prepare to defend against them, ensuring the protection of their assets, data, and overall integrity.

How to Integrate BDOs Effectively

Effective integration of Behaviour Detection Officers (BDOs) is crucial to a BDM's success. BDOs serve as the first line of defence, observing human behaviour in real-time and reporting suspicious activities. To ensure these officers function cohesively within the broader security framework, the BDM must provide clear instructions and facilitate ongoing communication between team members.

Here are key responsibilities for managing BDOs:

1. **Training and Development:** BDOs must receive continuous training to stay up-to-date on the latest behaviour detection techniques. A well-trained team can better identify threats and avoid mistakes.
2. **Clear Communication:** Establishing streamlined communication channels ensures that BDOs can quickly report suspicious behaviour to the BDM, who can then escalate the matter if necessary.
3. **Coordination with Other Security Teams:** BDOs must work in concert with other teams, such as CCTV operators, security guards, and cyber surveillance units. The BDM ensures these teams collaborate to prevent gaps in the security network.
4. **Debriefing and Feedback:** After an incident, the BDM leads debriefings to evaluate the effectiveness of the response, highlight successes, and identify areas for improvement.

Environmental Awareness and Operational Strategies

Environmental awareness is critical for a BDM. Every environment presents unique challenges, and the behaviour detection strategy must be tailored to suit the specific location—whether that's an airport, a corporate office, or a public venue.

- **Airports** require heightened vigilance because of the large number of transient individuals and the high risk of terrorism.
- **Corporate offices** may be more focused on preventing insider threats or corporate espionage.
- **Public venues**, like malls or stadiums, demand a broader approach to monitor both insider and external threats.

For instance:

As a BDM, it's essential to know the operational environment intimately:

1. **Identify Vulnerable Points:** Every location has areas where security may be more vulnerable, such as entry and exit points, high-traffic zones, and areas out of camera view.
2. **Tailor Operational Plans:** Customize your approach to address the specific needs of the environment.
3. **Utilize Technology Effectively:** Combine technology, like CCTV or facial recognition software, with human observation to create a comprehensive security system.

Legal and Ethical Considerations: How Far Can You Go?

One of the most challenging aspects of being a BDM is navigating legal and ethical considerations. While behaviour detection is vital, actions must be compliant with the law and ethical standards to avoid overreach.

Key considerations include:

- **Privacy Laws:** Different countries have various regulations around monitoring individuals. A BDM must ensure their operations comply with privacy laws and avoid unnecessary surveillance or data collection.
- **Avoiding Bias and Discrimination:** It's essential that BDOs are trained to detect suspicious behaviour based on objective factors, not subjective biases such as race, ethnicity, or personal appearance.
- **Use of Force:** The BDM must ensure that force or detention is only used when necessary and in accordance with the law.

Managing Threat Response: Escalation and Crisis Management

One of the most critical aspects of a BDM's role is managing a response once a potential threat is detected. Proper escalation procedures ensure that suspicious behaviour is handled quickly and effectively, minimizing the risk to people and property.

Steps for managing a threat response include:

1. **Assessment of the Threat:** Is this a low-level threat that can be managed with simple questioning, or is immediate intervention required?
2. **Coordination of Resources:** Depending on the situation, the BDM may need to coordinate efforts between different teams, including law enforcement or emergency services.
3. **Communication:** Keeping upper management and security teams informed is essential during any escalation process.
4. **Post-Incident Debriefing:** After the threat is neutralized, a debrief should be conducted to identify what went well and what could be improved in future incidents.

Scenario 1: Suspicious Individual at an Airport – What to Do

Setting: An international airport is bustling with passengers. A BDO notices a middle-aged man exhibiting strange behaviour—pacing nervously, avoiding eye contact with security personnel, and frequently glancing toward the exits.

Actions Taken:

- The BDO discretely observes and reports the man's behaviour.
- Approaching the individual, the BDO asks non-intrusive questions and requests identification.
- The man's nervous responses and inconsistent travel documents lead the BDO to escalate the matter to the BDM.
- The BDM coordinates with law enforcement to intercept the individual before he clears security.

Why It Works: This example illustrates the importance of proper observation, measured questioning, and timely escalation. The BDO handled the situation without alarming nearby passengers, and the BDM ensured swift action by coordinating with law enforcement.

Scenario 2: False Alarm in a Corporate Setting – What Not to Do

Setting: In a corporate office, a BDO notices a long-time employee behaving differently than usual—avoiding eye contact and not engaging with others. Without further observation, the BDO confronts the employee and escalates the situation to the BDM, resulting in an embarrassing false alarm.

Actions Taken:

- The BDO overreacts by confronting the employee prematurely.
- The BDM escalates the situation without gathering enough evidence or observing additional behaviour.

Why It Fails: This scenario highlights the dangers of overreacting. The BDO should have observed the employee over a longer period, and the BDM should have required more evidence before escalating the situation. Instead, the hasty response damaged trust and caused unnecessary disruption.

Scenario 3: Coordinated Hostile Reconnaissance – What to Do as a BDM

Setting: A BDO at a major shopping mall has noticed something troubling over the course of a few days. A group of three men have been visiting the mall regularly, each taking photos in unusual locations: near security checkpoints, exit routes, and high-traffic areas. The men rarely shop and seem to be more interested in the layout of the building.

Actions Taken:

- The BDO reports detailed observations to the BDM.
- The BDM instructs the BDO to continue surveillance and reviews CCTV footage.
- The BDM coordinates with law enforcement, providing them with all available evidence, including video footage, times of visits, and descriptions. This ensures that the professionals equipped to handle serious threats can take over if necessary.

Why It Works: The BDM's decision to gather evidence before taking action ensures that the situation is handled calmly and without causing unnecessary alarm. By involving law enforcement early, the BDM ensures that all legal bases are covered and that any potentially dangerous activity is stopped in its tracks. This scenario highlights the importance of patience, observation, and proper coordination in behaviour detection.

Scenario 4: Internal Threat – Handling a Suspicious Package

Setting: You are the BDM in charge of security at a financial institution. A BDO on routine patrol notices a suspicious package near an office exit that no one appears to claim. The BDO remembers the training on suspicious items and immediately follows protocol, alerting you to the situation.

Actions Taken:

- The BDO alerts the BDM, who orders the area to be cleared.
- Following your organization's security protocol, you initiate the procedure for handling suspicious packages. You alert the relevant authorities—either bomb disposal units or local law enforcement—without attempting to handle the package yourself.
- If law enforcement determines that the package poses a legitimate threat, you coordinate a controlled evacuation, ensuring the safety of employees and customers. As a BDM, your responsibility is not only to manage detection but also to oversee response and crisis management.

Why It Works: By following a clear protocol, the BDM and BDO maintain control over the situation, minimizing risk and avoiding panic. The key to success here is measured, deliberate action based on training and established guidelines. Both the BDM and the BDO work in tandem to ensure the safety of the organization without escalating unnecessarily.

Concluding Thoughts

A BDM's role is about far more than just managing people. It's about understanding threats, coordinating responses, and ensuring that every action taken is both legally compliant and ethically sound. With a focus on real-world examples, we've demonstrated how the principles of behaviour detection can be applied to manage risks effectively.

Chapter 2: Behaviour Detection Officer (BDO)

The Frontline Role: A Day in the Life of a Behaviour Detection Officer

While the Behaviour Detection Manager (BDM) sets the strategic direction, the Behaviour Detection Officer (BDO) is the key operative on the ground, responsible for real-time observations of individuals. A BDO's role involves constant vigilance, recognizing and reporting suspicious behaviours while remaining discreet and professional.

Key Responsibilities of a BDO

1. **Observation and Detection:**
   BDOs must constantly observe people within their assigned environment, looking for unusual or suspicious behaviours. This includes reading body language, facial expressions, movement patterns, and other signs that may indicate someone is acting with malicious intent. The officer must recognize subtle differences between normal human behaviour and signs of potential danger, such as nervousness, evasiveness, or reluctance to engage with security measures.

2. **Engagement and Interaction:**
   Once a BDO identifies a person exhibiting suspicious behaviour, they need to engage that person calmly and professionally. This involves asking non-threatening questions, reading their responses, and deciding if further action is necessary. For instance, if someone avoids eye contact while being questioned about their purpose in the area, the BDO may need to ask follow-up questions or check their identification to verify their legitimacy.

3. **Reporting and Escalation:**

A crucial aspect of the BDO's role is knowing when and how to escalate a situation to the Behaviour Detection Manager (BDM) or law enforcement. If, after engaging with the individual, the BDO still perceives a threat, they must promptly communicate their findings to higher authorities for further investigation or intervention. Detailed and accurate reporting is vital in ensuring the right action is taken.

4. **Team Collaboration:**

BDOs don't operate in isolation. They work alongside other security personnel, including CCTV operators, security guards, and cyber surveillance teams. Their ability to collaborate effectively and share timely information ensures that the security apparatus functions as a cohesive unit.

5. **Environmental Awareness:**

The effectiveness of a BDO also depends on their familiarity with the environment they are tasked to monitor. Whether it's an airport, a corporate office, or a public venue, BDOs must understand the baseline behaviours typical to that setting. Recognizing what is "normal" in any given environment allows the officer to identify anomalies more efficiently.

Behavioural Detection Techniques: What to Look For

The following are common behavioural indicators that may suggest malicious intent or the need for further investigation:

1. **Nervousness and Anxiety:**
   Individuals involved in criminal activities or planning an attack often exhibit signs of anxiety, such as excessive sweating, fidgeting, or avoiding eye contact. While nervousness can have innocent explanations, a BDO is trained to differentiate between natural anxiety and behaviour that raises red flags.

2. **Evasive or Defensive Behaviour:**
   Someone who tries to avoid security checks or offers vague answers when questioned about their purpose may warrant closer attention. Evasive actions, such as turning away from security personnel or making an abrupt change in direction, are often pre-attack indicators.

3. **Unusual Interest in Security Measures:**
   Individuals who take a keen interest in the layout of security checkpoints, the number of security personnel, or the positioning of CCTV cameras may be conducting hostile reconnaissance.

4. **Inconsistent or Inappropriate Clothing:**
   BDOs are trained to notice inconsistencies in attire, such as bulky clothing on a warm day, which may indicate the concealment of weapons or explosives.

5. **Unusual Access Attempts:**
   A person attempting to enter restricted areas without authorization or behaving suspiciously around secure doors or gates should be immediately flagged.

Scenario 1: Suspicious Behaviour at a Public Event

Setting:

A large outdoor concert is taking place in a major city. Thousands of attendees are passing through the security gates. A BDO stationed at one of the gates notices a man standing near the entrance, repeatedly glancing at the security personnel but making no move to enter.

What the BDO Does:

- The BDO continues observing the man's behaviour, noting his apparent nervousness and reluctance to approach the security checkpoint.
- After a few minutes, the BDO discreetly approaches the man and engages in conversation. "Good afternoon, sir. Are you heading inside for the concert?" This friendly approach gives the officer a chance to gauge the man's reactions up close.
- The man seems startled and mumbles something about waiting for a friend, but continues to glance at the security checkpoint. The BDO notices the man is wearing a large jacket, despite the warm weather.
- The BDO asks a few more questions, including a request for identification. The man becomes increasingly defensive, refusing to provide any ID.
- Recognizing this behaviour as highly suspicious, the BDO alerts the BDM, who instructs security to intercept the individual for further questioning.

Outcome:

Upon further investigation, it's revealed the man was carrying a concealed weapon. Thanks to the BDO's vigilance and measured response, a potential attack was prevented.

Lessons Learned:
This scenario highlights the importance of combining observational skills with non-threatening engagement. The BDO didn't escalate the situation prematurely but gathered enough information to make an informed decision about escalation.

Scenario 2: Overreaction and the Consequences

Setting:
A corporate building during the middle of the workday. A BDO on patrol notices an employee behaving strangely in the lobby—walking quickly and avoiding eye contact with others. The employee is carrying a large bag that seems out of place in an office environment.

What the BDO Does Wrong:

- The BDO immediately confronts the employee without further observation or context, assuming the bag could contain a threat.
- In a loud voice, the BDO demands to see the contents of the bag, attracting the attention of other employees nearby.
- The employee, startled and embarrassed, explains that they were simply in a rush to catch a meeting and were carrying a personal item. The bag contains gym clothes.

Outcome:
The BDO's overreaction causes unnecessary panic and disrupts the office environment. While it's important to be vigilant, the BDO failed to gather enough information before confronting the individual, leading to a false alarm.

Lessons Learned:
In this case, the BDO jumped to conclusions without following proper procedure. A calmer, more measured approach—such as observing the employee's actions over a longer period or asking neutral questions—could have prevented an embarrassing situation.

The Psychological Side of Detection: Understanding Human Behaviour

A BDO's work goes beyond mere observation. They must have a deep understanding of human psychology and how emotions like fear, guilt, or stress manifest in behaviour. This requires emotional intelligence and the ability to interpret body language, tone of voice, and subtle cues that might indicate deception or malicious intent.

Key psychological insights a BDO should consider include:

- **The Flight Response:** People under stress often exhibit the fight-or-flight response. BDOs need to watch for signs of the flight response—such as fidgeting, excessive blinking, or hurried movements—that indicate the individual is anxious or wants to leave the scene quickly.
- **Micro-Expressions:** Sometimes, people can mask their true emotions, but brief, involuntary facial expressions (micro-expressions) can reveal underlying feelings of fear, anger, or guilt. These fleeting expressions can provide valuable insight into an individual's state of mind.
- **Vocal Cues:** Changes in a person's tone, pitch, or speech pattern when questioned may indicate nervousness or deception. A BDO should pay attention to these vocal cues, especially when an individual seems evasive or unsure of their answers.

Effective Engagement: Asking the Right Questions

When engaging with a suspicious individual, the way questions are framed can significantly impact the outcome of the interaction. A BDO should avoid aggressive or confrontational questioning, which may escalate the situation. Instead, neutral, open-ended questions that encourage conversation are more effective. Examples include:

- "Do you need any help today?"
- "Are you waiting for someone?"
- "I noticed you've been in this area for a while. Is everything alright?"

These questions allow the BDO to gauge the person's reaction without making them feel threatened, giving the officer more information to assess the situation.

Scenario 3: Recognizing Malicious Insider Behaviour

Setting:

A high-security facility with restricted access areas. A BDO notices an employee entering and exiting a restricted area multiple times during the day, which is unusual for their role.

What the BDO Does:

- The BDO discreetly observes the employee over several hours, noting their frequent movements in and out of secure areas.
- Without raising alarm, the BDO checks the employee's clearance level and finds that their access to the restricted area is limited.
- The BDO reports their observations to the BDM, who coordinates with IT to review the employee's access logs. It turns out the employee has been accessing sensitive data outside their clearance level.
- Further investigation reveals the employee was attempting to steal proprietary information for a competitor.

Outcome:

The combined vigilance of the BDO and BDM prevented a serious security breach. By observing the employee over time and gathering evidence before taking action, the BDO avoided raising suspicion and tipping off the insider.

Lessons Learned:

This scenario demonstrates the importance of patience, observation, and discreet investigation. A BDO must resist the urge to jump to conclusions and instead follow a systematic approach to confirm their suspicions before escalating the situation.

Concluding Thoughts

The role of the Behaviour Detection Officer (BDO) is critical to any security operation. BDOs must strike a delicate balance between vigilance and discretion, knowing when to act and when to observe. By mastering techniques of behavioural observation, engagement, and escalation, BDOs serve as the first line of defence against potential threats.

Chapter 3: Behaviour Detection Awareness (BDA)

Foundations of Behaviour Detection Awareness: Why It Matters for Security

While the Behaviour Detection Manager (BDM) and Behaviour Detection Officers (BDOs) take the lead on threat detection, every employee within an organization can contribute to security through Behaviour Detection Awareness (BDA). A well-implemented BDA program ensures that everyone is trained to recognize and report suspicious behaviours, creating a culture of vigilance.

The primary goal of BDA is to equip non-security personnel with the knowledge and tools needed to identify potential threats early. This training ensures that all employees become an extension of the security team, contributing to the overall safety of the organization.

The Benefits of a Behaviour Detection Awareness Program

1. **Increased Early Detection:**
   By training all employees to recognize behavioural cues, the organization increases the chances of detecting a threat early, before it escalates into a serious situation.
2. **Reduced False Alarms:**
   A properly trained workforce can better distinguish between harmless behaviour and genuine threats, reducing the likelihood of unnecessary escalations or disruptions.
3. **Empowered Employees:**
   Employees who understand their role in maintaining security are more likely to report suspicious activities and feel a sense of responsibility toward the safety of the workplace.
4. **Creating a Security Culture:**
   BDA fosters an environment where security is a shared responsibility. When everyone understands the importance of behaviour detection, the organization becomes more resilient to threats.

Recognizing the 4 Stages of an Attack

Behaviour detection isn't limited to observing single moments of suspicious behaviour. It involves understanding the full context of an attack and recognizing the different stages an attacker typically goes through before launching their assault. These stages include:

1. **Surveillance:**

Attackers often begin by observing their target from a distance. This could involve studying security measures, noting the number of guards, or analyzing the flow of people through certain areas.

2. **Planning:**

Once the attacker gathers enough information, they move on to the planning phase. They may make multiple visits to the location, take photos, or test the response time of security personnel.

3. **Execution:**

The actual attack is the culmination of all previous stages. However, with effective BDA training, employees may notice signs of the earlier stages and report them before the attacker can execute their plan.

4. **Escape or Concealment:**

After an attack, the perpetrator may attempt to escape or blend in with the crowd to avoid capture. Employees trained in BDA are more likely to notice unusual behaviour during this phase and report it to security.

Scenario 1: Recognizing Pre-Attack Indicators

Setting:

A receptionist at a corporate headquarters notices a visitor who asks a series of odd questions about the building's security measures, including the number of guards, the position of surveillance cameras, and access points for delivery personnel.

What the Receptionist Does:

- The receptionist recalls her Behaviour Detection Awareness training and notes that the visitor's questions are unusual and focused on the building's security vulnerabilities.
- Rather than answering the questions directly, the receptionist asks the visitor to wait while she alerts security.
- Security personnel review CCTV footage and notice the visitor has been in the building before, asking similar questions. The individual is flagged for further investigation.

Outcome:

The receptionist's BDA training allowed her to recognize early signs of hostile reconnaissance. By alerting security promptly, the organization was able to prevent a potential threat.

Practical Training for Employees: What to Look For

Even employees with limited security responsibilities can be taught to recognize basic behavioural cues. These include:

- **Unusual Nervousness:**
  Sweating, fidgeting, or an inability to make eye contact may signal that someone is under stress or hiding something.
- **Odd or Inconsistent Behaviour:**
  Individuals acting out of character for the setting—such as someone who seems overly anxious at a routine business meeting—may be worth noting.
- **Surveillance Indicators:**
  People who take an unusual interest in security features, like cameras, guards, or restricted areas, may be conducting pre-attack reconnaissance.

Reporting Suspicious Behaviour: How to Empower Employees

A critical part of any Behaviour Detection Awareness program is teaching employees how to report suspicious behaviour effectively. This means ensuring that:

1. **There is a clear reporting protocol:**
   Employees should know exactly who to report to, whether that's their immediate supervisor, security personnel, or a hotline.
2. **Reports are taken seriously:**
   Management must emphasize that all reports will be investigated thoroughly, and employees should never feel that their concerns are being dismissed.
3. **Discretion is encouraged:**
   Employees should understand the importance of reporting suspicious behaviour discreetly to avoid alarming others or tipping off the individual in question.

Scenario 2: Behaviour Detection in a Retail Setting

Setting:
A department store employee notices a customer wandering around the store without purchasing anything. The customer seems unusually interested in the store's security cameras, frequently glancing up at them while moving through different sections of the store.

What the Employee Does:

- The employee recalls their BDA training and discreetly informs store security about the customer's unusual behaviour.
- Security personnel review CCTV footage and confirm the customer has been in the store on several previous occasions, each time exhibiting the same behaviour.
- The customer is intercepted by security, who discover they had been planning to steal high-value merchandise during busy hours.

Outcome:

Thanks to the store employee's training, a potential theft was prevented. This scenario highlights the importance of BDA training in non-corporate environments like retail, where employees may come into contact with individuals engaged in criminal activities.

Scenario 3: Recognizing Cyber Threat Indicators

Setting:

An IT employee at a large corporation notices that a colleague is accessing sensitive files outside of their clearance level and at odd hours. Although the colleague works in a different department, they seem to be interested in files related to a project they are not involved in.

What the IT Employee Does:

- The IT employee remembers their BDA training and notes that the colleague's behaviour is out of the ordinary.
- They report the unusual activity to their supervisor, who initiates an investigation.
- The investigation reveals the colleague had been attempting to steal proprietary information for a competitor.

Outcome:

The IT employee's vigilance helped prevent a major security breach. This scenario demonstrates that behaviour detection applies not only to physical environments but also to digital spaces.

Creating a Culture of Vigilance

One of the most powerful outcomes of a Behaviour Detection Awareness program is the development of a security-conscious culture. When employees understand the importance of behaviour detection and feel empowered to act, they create a safer environment for everyone.

Here are key steps to creating a culture of vigilance:

- **Regular Training:**
  BDA programs should not be a one-time event. Regular training sessions ensure that employees remain up-to-date on the latest behaviour detection techniques.
- **Positive Reinforcement:**
  Management should reward employees who report suspicious activity, reinforcing the idea that vigilance is valued.
- **Clear Communication Channels:**
  Ensure that all employees know how and where to report suspicious behaviour, whether through a direct supervisor, an internal hotline, or security personnel.

Behaviour Detection Awareness (BDA) transforms employees into active participants in maintaining security. By training staff to recognize and report suspicious behaviour, organizations can prevent threats before they materialize. In the next chapter, we will explore the role of technology in threat detection, focusing on Threat Image Recognition Training (TIRT) and how it enhances the effectiveness of X-ray screening operations.

Chapter 4: Threat Image Recognition Training (TIRT) 3D & 2D

The Evolving Landscape of Security Screening

As technological advancements continue to shape the security industry, Threat Image Recognition Training (TIRT) has become an essential part of ensuring that personnel remain highly skilled in detecting potential threats. X-ray screening systems are widely used to detect prohibited items in high-risk environments such as airports, government buildings, and corporate headquarters. While technology plays a pivotal role, it is the human element—trained screeners—that remains the most critical component in identifying potential threats.

This chapter delves into the importance of TIRT, the difference between 2D and 3D imaging technologies, and how human operators must work alongside these systems to maximize security outcomes. We will explore case studies of successful threat detection, along with scenarios that illustrate the challenges faced by screeners in real-world situations.

Understanding Threat Image Recognition Training (TIRT)

Threat Image Recognition Training (TIRT) is designed to sharpen the skills of security personnel by simulating real-world scenarios in which they must detect weapons, explosives, or other dangerous objects hidden in baggage or packages. While technology can automatically flag certain objects, it is the human operator's judgment and experience that play a decisive role in determining whether an item poses a threat.

Why is TIRT so important?

- **Accuracy:**
  Training personnel to recognize threats in X-ray images reduces the likelihood of human error, such as missing an item or misinterpreting an innocent object as dangerous.
- **Speed:**
  A well-trained screener can process images quickly, ensuring that security checkpoints remain efficient and do not cause unnecessary delays.
- **Confidence:**
  Operators who regularly undergo TIRT are more confident in their ability to make correct decisions under pressure, reducing false alarms and improving the overall security process.

TIRT programs usually include both theoretical training—where operators are introduced to various types of weapons, explosives, and prohibited items—and practical exercises that involve analyzing real or simulated X-ray images.

2D vs. 3D Image Recognition: Understanding the Differences

The transition from 2D to 3D imaging technologies has revolutionized the field of X-ray screening. Each has its advantages, and understanding the differences between these two approaches helps operators maximize their effectiveness in detecting threats.

1. **2D Image Recognition:**

   o **Flat Representation:** 2D X-ray images present a flat, two-dimensional view of an object. While this is useful for basic identification, it may not show the full depth of an object or how its components are arranged.
   o **Challenges:** Security personnel must interpret overlapping items in a 2D image, which can lead to difficulties in distinguishing between benign and dangerous items. For example, an electronic device like a laptop could obscure a prohibited item such as a knife.
   o **Training Requirement:** In 2D image recognition, screeners require extensive training to recognize the shape and structure of dangerous objects, even when these are partially obscured by other items.
   o

3D Image Recognition:

Depth and Perspective: 3D X-ray images allow operators to see objects from multiple angles, providing a more complete picture of the contents of a bag or package. This technology helps overcome the limitations of 2D images by providing more accurate visual data.

Precision: 3D imaging systems make it easier for screeners to identify complex items or items that may be partially hidden behind other objects. By rotating the object within the virtual space, screeners can view it from different perspectives and better assess the risk.

Training Requirement: Even with 3D technology, operators still need thorough training to interpret the data correctly. While 3D systems reduce the margin for error, they do not eliminate the need for human judgment.

Scenario 1: The Importance of Image Recognition Skills

Setting:

An international airport's security checkpoint. A BDO monitoring the X-ray screening system spots a suspicious image in a passenger's carry-on luggage. The system has flagged the image for manual review, and it's up to the screener to determine whether the item is dangerous.

What Happens:

- The screener notes that the image contains a dense object that could potentially be a weapon. The object is partially obscured by electronic devices, making it difficult to see clearly.
- Using their TIRT training, the screener decides to inspect the bag further rather than dismissing the item as benign. Upon closer examination, the screener finds that the object is, in fact, a dismantled firearm hidden within a laptop case.

Outcome:

Thanks to the screener's training and careful decision-making, a serious threat was neutralized before the passenger could board the flight.

Lessons Learned:

This scenario highlights the importance of TIRT in enhancing a screener's ability to detect complex threats, even when they are obscured by other objects in 2D images. The screener's training enabled them to differentiate between harmless items and components of a weapon.

Scenario 2: How 3D Technology Enhances Detection

Setting:

A high-security corporate office uses 3D X-ray imaging at its main entrance to screen all incoming deliveries. A security officer is responsible for reviewing images of packages delivered to the building.

What Happens:

- A package arrives that, on first glance, appears to contain office supplies. However, the 3D imaging system reveals that within the box, an object is partially hidden beneath layers of paper.
- The screener rotates the image using the 3D interface and notices that the object has a shape consistent with a small explosive device. The package is flagged for further inspection, and the building's security protocol is activated.

Outcome:

The 3D system, combined with the screener's training, allowed the team to detect an explosive device before it reached its intended target inside the building. The package was safely removed and dealt with by the appropriate authorities.

Lessons Learned:

3D imaging technology enhances an operator's ability to spot hidden or camouflaged items that might go unnoticed in a 2D system. This scenario shows how combining technology with TIRT training creates a robust security system capable of detecting even sophisticated threats.

Human Judgment: The Key Component in Screening Operations

While advanced imaging technologies provide significant advantages in threat detection, human judgment remains the most important element in screening operations. Machines can flag potentially dangerous items, but they cannot always make the final call. Human operators must interpret the data, ask critical questions, and make decisions based on a combination of technology and intuition.

Human Factors in Screening:

- **Fatigue and Attention Span:**
  X-ray screening is a demanding job that requires intense concentration. Over time, screeners can experience fatigue, leading to lapses in judgment. Regular TIRT sessions help keep skills sharp and reduce the likelihood of human error.
- **Bias and Perception:**
  It's important for screeners to avoid biases when analyzing X-ray images. Assumptions based on appearance, age, or gender can lead to misjudgments. TIRT emphasizes the importance of focusing solely on the contents of the image, not on who is carrying the item.
- **Speed vs. Accuracy:**
  There is often pressure to process large numbers of passengers or packages quickly, especially in busy environments like airports. TIRT helps screeners strike a balance between speed and accuracy, ensuring that no threats are overlooked in the rush to clear security checkpoints.

Case Study: Successful Threat Detection Using TIRT

Setting:

An international cargo facility responsible for screening packages destined for high-security locations.

The Incident:

A cargo handler notices that several packages have been sent from the same location over the course of a week, each containing innocuous items like office supplies and household goods. The handler flags this as unusual and alerts the TIRT-trained screeners.

Upon closer inspection using 3D X-ray imaging, one of the packages is revealed to contain concealed wiring and components that resemble an improvised explosive device (IED). The package is immediately removed from circulation, and law enforcement is notified.

Outcome:

The combination of human vigilance and advanced X-ray imaging systems, supported by regular TIRT training, prevented the delivery of a potentially deadly device to a secure location.

Lessons Learned:

This case study demonstrates the importance of integrating technology with well-trained human operators. Without the handler's observation and the screener's skills in interpreting complex images, the threat might have gone undetected.

Scenario 3: Avoiding False Positives

Setting:

A high-traffic airport where thousands of passengers pass through daily. A screener spots a suspicious object in a passenger's bag—a dense, metallic shape that appears to be a knife.

What Happens:

- The screener alerts security and stops the passenger for further questioning.
- Upon closer inspection, it's revealed that the object is a harmless souvenir—a decorative item that only resembled a weapon in the X-ray image.
- While the false positive caused a temporary delay, the screener followed protocol correctly by flagging the suspicious object for inspection.

Lessons Learned:

False positives are an inevitable part of threat detection. However, with proper training, screeners can minimize the impact of these false alarms by efficiently verifying the nature of the item and clearing passengers or packages with minimal disruption.

Continuous Improvement Through TIRT: Keeping Skills Sharp

The dynamic nature of security threats means that screeners and security personnel must constantly improve their skills. TIRT is not a one-time training but an ongoing process of skill enhancement. Regular training sessions help screeners stay updated on:

- **New types of threats:**
  As criminals develop new methods to bypass security, screeners must be trained to recognize innovative ways to hide weapons, explosives, and other prohibited items.
- **Technological advances:**
  As 3D and AI-assisted screening technologies evolve, operators need to learn how to use these tools effectively.
- **Real-world simulations:**
  By engaging in simulations that mimic real-world threats, screeners can test their skills in a controlled environment and receive feedback on their performance.

Concluding Thoughts

Threat Image Recognition Training (TIRT) is a critical part of any organization's security strategy. While technology such as 2D and 3D imaging systems provides powerful tools for detecting threats, it is the human element—well-trained screeners—that ultimately determines the success or failure of a security operation. By investing in regular TIRT, organizations ensure that their personnel are equipped to handle the most sophisticated threats, keeping people and property safe from harm.

Chapter 5: Behaviour Detection Techniques and Application

Course Overview: Understanding the Art and Science of Behaviour Detection

Behaviour detection has evolved significantly over the years, becoming an integral part of modern security strategies. The aim is to identify suspicious activities or individuals through the observation of behavioural cues before a threat materializes. In this chapter, we'll explore a comprehensive range of behaviour detection techniques, focusing on how to apply them in real-world scenarios, the legal considerations that guide these efforts, and the recent developments in behaviour detection, such as the introduction of *Martyn's Law* and its implications for security personnel.

This chapter also highlights the role that Behaviour Detection Officers (BDOs) play in observing, assessing, and responding to potential threats. We will examine practical case studies that illustrate how these techniques have been applied to successfully mitigate risks, as well as scenarios where ineffective application led to missed opportunities for intervention.

Introduction to Behaviour Detection: From Baselines to Anomalies

Behaviour detection hinges on the principle of identifying deviations from the norm, known as *baselines*. A baseline refers to the standard or typical behaviour expected in a given environment. For example, the way people behave at an airport is quite different from how they might act in a shopping mall or corporate office. To detect suspicious behaviour, a Behaviour Detection Officer (BDO) must first understand the baseline for the specific environment they are working in.

Once a baseline is established, the officer can focus on identifying *anomalies*—behaviour that deviates from the norm. This could include someone loitering in a restricted area, appearing overly nervous, or taking an unusual interest in the security infrastructure of a location.

The Key Components of Behaviour Detection

1. **Baseline Understanding:**
   Each environment has its own set of typical behaviours. An airport, for instance, sees a lot of hurried travellers, people checking their phones, and individuals focused on catching their flights. In contrast, a corporate office may have a more relaxed atmosphere, with employees casually interacting with one another. A BDO's effectiveness depends on their ability to differentiate between normal and suspicious behaviour based on the environment.

2. **Identifying Anomalies:**
   Behaviour that stands out as unusual in a particular setting often signals the need for closer attention. For instance, in an airport, someone who is pacing near the security checkpoint but not attempting to pass through may be considered an anomaly. Similarly, an employee in a corporate setting who suddenly starts accessing restricted areas without authorization is another example of suspicious behaviour.

3. **Contextual Cues:**
Anomalies alone don't always indicate a threat. Behaviour detection relies on context. An individual sweating profusely may not be a threat if they are just nervous about flying. However, if that individual also avoids eye contact with security personnel, frequently checks their surroundings, and carries a suspicious item, their behaviour becomes more concerning. BDOs must always consider the broader context when assessing potential threats.

Techniques for Effective Behaviour Detection

1. **The Art of Observation:**
Observation is the foundation of behaviour detection. BDOs must have a heightened sense of awareness, constantly scanning their environment for anything out of the ordinary. This includes noticing body language, facial expressions, and even tone of voice.

   o Key indicators to observe include:

     - Unusual nervousness or anxiety, such as fidgeting, sweating, or avoiding eye contact.
     - Body language that indicates a lack of confidence, discomfort, or excessive caution.
     - Movements or actions that seem out of place for the environment, such as lingering too long in one area without a clear purpose.

2. **Non-Threatening Engagement:**

   Once a BDO identifies suspicious behaviour, the next step is to engage the individual in a non-threatening manner. The aim is to gather more information without escalating the situation. Open-ended questions, such as "Do you need assistance?" or "Can I help you find something?" are useful for gauging the person's reaction.

   The individual's response—both verbal and non-verbal—can provide further insights. For example, if the person seems startled or defensive when approached, this could be a red flag.

3. **Baseline and Deviation Technique:**

   BDOs often use the *Baseline and Deviation* technique, which involves mentally cataloguing typical behaviour in their environment and comparing it to any deviations they observe. This technique requires patience and keen observation, as deviations may only appear after extended observation. A person might seem normal at first but start exhibiting unusual behaviour over time.

4. **Challenge and Response:**

   The *Challenge and Response* method is used to further assess an individual's intentions. If someone is behaving suspiciously, the BDO may ask them a direct question—challenging them in a calm and controlled manner. The individual's response will help the BDO determine whether their behaviour is innocent or if further action is needed.

   For example, asking a person lingering near a restricted area, "Excuse me, do you have a pass for this section?" will help reveal whether their presence is legitimate or if they are attempting to access a secure zone improperly.

Scenario 1: Suspicious Behaviour in a Public Space

Setting:

A Behaviour Detection Officer (BDO) is stationed at a busy shopping mall. The officer notices a man lingering near the mall's security office for an extended period. The man avoids eye contact with the BDO and repeatedly checks his phone.

What Happens:

- The BDO observes the man's behaviour and notes that it deviates from the baseline. Most mall visitors move quickly through the area, while this individual seems unusually focused on the security office.
- The BDO decides to engage the individual, asking, "Excuse me, can I help you with something?"
- The man appears startled and offers a vague answer, claiming he's waiting for someone. He continues to act nervously, frequently glancing at the security office.
- The BDO escalates the situation to the BDM, who reviews security footage. Upon further investigation, it is revealed that the man had been conducting hostile reconnaissance, gathering information about the mall's security layout in preparation for a planned attack.

Outcome:

The BDO's ability to observe deviations from normal behaviour and respond appropriately helped prevent a serious security incident. By staying calm and using the Challenge and Response technique, the BDO gathered enough information to escalate the matter for further investigation.

Scenario 2: Overcoming Bias in Behaviour Detection

Setting:

An airport security checkpoint during a busy travel day. A BDO notices a middle-aged man with a large backpack looking anxious and sweating as he waits in line for security. The officer begins to monitor the man's behaviour, noting that he seems to be avoiding eye contact with security personnel.

What Happens:

- The BDO continues to observe the man but keeps in mind that nervousness alone is not necessarily an indicator of malicious intent.
- Rather than immediately escalating the situation, the BDO engages the man in conversation, asking, "Are you alright, sir? It looks like you're a bit stressed."
- The man explains that he has a fear of flying, which accounts for his nervous behaviour. After providing reassurance, the BDO observes that the man's behaviour begins to normalize as he progresses through security.

Outcome:

In this case, the BDO avoided making assumptions based solely on the individual's appearance and initial anxiety. Instead, they used engagement and contextual observation to determine that the man was not a threat. This scenario underscores the importance of avoiding bias and basing decisions on a broader set of behavioural cues.

Legal and Ethical Considerations in Behaviour Detection

While behaviour detection is essential for maintaining security, it must always be carried out within the bounds of legal and ethical guidelines. Overstepping these boundaries can lead to violations of privacy, false accusations, and damage to an organization's reputation. Security personnel must be trained to operate within the law while still effectively identifying and mitigating potential threats.

1. **Privacy Concerns:**
   Behaviour detection often involves observing individuals in public or semi-public spaces. However, it's important to avoid infringing on personal privacy rights. BDOs should ensure that their actions remain within legal limits, such as avoiding unnecessary surveillance of individuals without cause.

2. **Avoiding Discrimination:**
   Behaviour detection should be based solely on observable actions and should never be influenced by racial, gender, or cultural biases. Officers must be trained to recognize that suspicious behaviour can occur in individuals of any background and that profiling based on appearance is both unethical and ineffective.

3. **Use of Force and Detention:**
   When escalating a situation, BDOs and BDMs must ensure that any use of force or detention is proportional to the threat and compliant with legal standards. Escalating too quickly or without sufficient evidence can lead to legal challenges.

Martyn's Law: The Legal Framework for Behaviour Detection

In recent years, the introduction of *Martyn's Law* has had a significant impact on the way behaviour detection is implemented, particularly in public venues. Martyn's Law, named after Martyn Hett, one of the victims of the 2017 Manchester Arena bombing, aims to increase the level of security at public venues to prevent future terrorist attacks.

Chapter 6: Hostile Reconnaissance and Security Awareness

Understanding Hostile Reconnaissance: The Foundation of Pre-Attack Planning

Hostile reconnaissance is a crucial phase in the planning of any criminal or terrorist attack. It involves the deliberate and methodical observation of a target to gather intelligence that will inform the planning and execution of the attack. Hostile actors engage in this reconnaissance to identify vulnerabilities, understand security measures, and determine the best time and method for carrying out their operation. For security professionals, detecting hostile reconnaissance early is essential to preventing attacks before they occur.

According to the National Protective Security Authority (NPSA), hostile reconnaissance is defined as "purposeful observation with the intention of collecting information to inform the planning of a hostile act against a specific target." This chapter delves into the various methods used by hostile actors to gather intelligence, the signs that security personnel should look for, and how to implement effective countermeasures.

The Four Stages of Hostile Reconnaissance

Hostile reconnaissance typically follows a structured process, with each stage bringing the attacker closer to executing their plan. These stages often mirror those of a typical surveillance operation but are tailored to identify weak points in a target's security measures.

1. **Target Selection:**

   In the initial stage, hostile actors will choose a potential target based on their goals. This could be a high-profile public venue, an important corporate facility, or an individual of significance. During this phase, attackers often conduct high-level, general observations from afar to assess the potential target's vulnerabilities.

2. **General Surveillance:**

   Once a target has been chosen, the next step is to gather more detailed information. Attackers will monitor the site over time, paying attention to security routines, access points, peak times, and potential weaknesses. They may visit the site multiple times under the guise of ordinary visitors, blending in with the public to avoid detection.

3. **Detailed Surveillance:**

   In this stage, attackers will start documenting specific security measures, noting any changes in routines and identifying personnel who might be obstacles to their plan. They may take photos, record videos, or sketch diagrams of the site's layout. Often, multiple individuals are involved in this phase, each assigned to observe different aspects of the target.

4. **Final Preparations:**

   With all the necessary intelligence gathered, the attackers enter the final stage of hostile reconnaissance. Here, they fine-tune their plan, possibly conducting rehearsals or "dry runs" to test their approach. The final preparations phase often includes acquiring any necessary equipment or disguises for the actual execution of the attack.

At each stage, there are specific indicators that security personnel, particularly Behaviour Detection Officers (BDOs), can look for to identify and disrupt the reconnaissance before it reaches the final stage.

Key Indicators of Hostile Reconnaissance

Hostile reconnaissance may not always be immediately apparent, especially when conducted by trained professionals. However, there are certain behaviours and activities that can signal reconnaissance is taking place. These indicators often involve patterns of suspicious activity or anomalies in behaviour that deviate from the norm for the given environment.

1. **Repeated Visits by the Same Individual(s):**
   A person visiting a site multiple times without a clear reason, especially at different times of the day, may be conducting reconnaissance. They may linger in areas that provide a good vantage point for observing security personnel or entry points.

2. **Unusual Interest in Security Measures:**
   Individuals who take an excessive interest in the placement of security cameras, guards, or emergency exits should be monitored closely. They may ask questions about security protocols or casually observe how the security team responds to routine operations.

3. **Use of Technology:**
   Hostile actors often use technology to aid their reconnaissance efforts. This could include taking photographs, recording video, or using smartphones or tablets to capture information. In some cases, they may use more sophisticated devices, such as hidden cameras or drones, to gather intelligence without drawing attention.

4. **Loitering and Lingering:**

People who loiter in a particular area for no apparent reason may be observing security patterns. They might pretend to be waiting for someone or browsing stores, but their true focus is on monitoring the site's vulnerabilities.

5. **Suspicious Questioning:**

Asking specific, security-related questions, such as "What time do the guards change shifts?" or "How often do you check the emergency exits?" can be a major red flag. Individuals engaging in hostile reconnaissance may attempt to extract information by posing as customers, tourists, or even employees.

6. **Disguises and Evasive Behaviours:**

Hostile actors may try to blend in with their surroundings by wearing disguises or changing their appearance during different visits. They may also avoid eye contact with security personnel, appear overly cautious, or behave nervously when approached.

Scenario 1: Identifying Hostile Reconnaissance at a Corporate Facility

Setting:

A Behaviour Detection Officer (BDO) working at a high-security corporate facility notices an individual standing outside the building several days in a row. The individual seems to be taking notes and occasionally using their phone to take pictures of the building's entry points.

What Happens:

- The BDO makes note of the individual's repeated presence and their interest in the building's security infrastructure.
- On the third day, the BDO approaches the individual under the guise of a friendly conversation. The officer asks if they need assistance or if they are lost.
- The individual offers vague answers and seems evasive, claiming to be a contractor working nearby, yet provides no specific details.
- The BDO escalates the situation to the Behaviour Detection Manager (BDM), who initiates a review of CCTV footage and confirms that the individual has been observing the building's security operations over the past week.
- Law enforcement is notified, and the individual is detained for further questioning, revealing that they were planning a corporate espionage operation.

Outcome:

By identifying the signs of hostile reconnaissance early, the BDO was able to prevent the gathering of sensitive information that could have compromised the company's security. The officer's proactive approach in engaging the individual allowed security to intervene before the reconnaissance advanced to the final stages.

Lessons Learned:

This scenario underscores the importance of early detection and engagement. Hostile reconnaissance often takes place over an extended period, so BDOs must remain vigilant for patterns of suspicious behaviour, even if it seems harmless at first.

Scenario 2: Hostile Reconnaissance at a Public Venue

Setting:

A major sports event is taking place at a stadium. A BDO monitoring the main entrance notices a group of individuals standing near a security checkpoint, appearing to study the movements of security guards and taking photos of the checkpoint from different angles.

What Happens:

- The BDO observes the group from a distance, noting their repeated focus on the security checkpoint. The individuals appear to be timing how long it takes for guards to rotate shifts and how thoroughly bags are searched.
- The BDO discreetly informs the Behaviour Detection Manager (BDM) of the situation, who instructs other BDOs to monitor the group's movements through the stadium's CCTV system.
- Upon reviewing the footage, the BDM sees that the individuals have visited the stadium multiple times over the past week, each time observing different entry points and security measures.
- Law enforcement is contacted, and the group is intercepted. Upon further investigation, it is revealed that the individuals were planning to exploit gaps in the stadium's security during a high-profile event.

Outcome:

The combined efforts of the BDO and BDM, along with the use of technology, successfully identified and disrupted the hostile reconnaissance before it could progress to an attack. The situation was handled discreetly, without causing alarm among the public.

Lessons Learned:

This scenario highlights the importance of collaboration between security personnel and the strategic use of technology, such as CCTV, to track suspicious individuals. It also emphasizes the need for patience in detecting patterns over time, as hostile reconnaissance often involves multiple visits to the target site.

Practical Techniques for Detecting Hostile Reconnaissance

1. **Situational Awareness:**

   BDOs must always maintain situational awareness of their surroundings, scanning the environment for anything that seems out of place. This includes monitoring high-risk areas such as entrances, exits, and security checkpoints, where hostile actors are likely to focus their attention.

2. **Suspicious Behaviour Profiling:**

   By creating a profile of suspicious behaviours based on previous incidents, security personnel can identify potential hostile reconnaissance activities early. This profile might include individuals who appear overly interested in security measures, engage in loitering, or visit the site multiple times without a clear purpose.

3. **Use of Technology:**

   Security systems such as CCTV, facial recognition software, and automatic license plate readers can be invaluable in identifying hostile reconnaissance. These tools help track individuals' movements and can alert security personnel to patterns of suspicious behaviour.

4. **Covert Monitoring:**

Hostile actors may be more cautious if they know they are being observed. Therefore, BDOs and other security personnel should consider covert monitoring strategies to gather information without alerting the individual. This could involve using plainclothes officers or remote surveillance techniques.

5. **Engagement and De-escalation:**

If a BDO suspects hostile reconnaissance, engaging the individual in conversation can provide valuable insights. However, it's important to approach these interactions calmly and without aggression to avoid escalating the situation unnecessarily. Simple, non-threatening questions can often prompt revealing responses.

Training Staff in Hostile Reconnaissance Awareness

While Behaviour Detection Officers (BDOs) and other security personnel are at the forefront of detecting hostile reconnaissance, all employees and staff at a facility should be trained to recognize the signs. Training programs on hostile reconnaissance and security awareness can greatly enhance an organization's ability to prevent attacks. These programs should include:

Recognizing Pre-Attack Indicators: Teaching staff to recognize the early signs of reconnaissance, such as individuals taking photos of security measures, asking unusual questions, or repeatedly visiting the site without a clear reason.

Understanding the Importance of Reporting: Staff should know how to report suspicious activity promptly and discreetly. Clear reporting channels must be established so that employees feel comfortable escalating concerns to security personnel.

Interactive Exercises and Tabletop Drills: Conducting tabletop exercises and interactive drills can help employees practice their response to hostile reconnaissance scenarios. These exercises provide a safe environment to test decision-making and collaboration between staff and security personnel.

Scenario 3: Training Reception Staff to Detect Hostile Reconnaissance

Setting:
A corporate office building has implemented hostile reconnaissance training for its reception staff. During the training, the staff learns how to recognize suspicious behaviours, such as visitors asking detailed questions about security procedures or attempting to access restricted areas.

What Happens:

- One day, a visitor arrives at the building and starts asking the receptionist about the security system, including how often guards patrol and whether any areas are left unattended.
- Thanks to her training, the receptionist immediately recognizes the questioning as a potential pre-attack indicator. She remains polite but provides no specific information. Instead, she discreetly informs the BDO stationed nearby.
- The BDO observes the visitor's behaviour, noting that they are lingering near the security desk and watching how employees use their access cards to enter restricted areas.
- The BDM is alerted, and the visitor is questioned further, eventually leading to the discovery that they were gathering intelligence for a future break-in.

Outcome:
The receptionist's training in hostile reconnaissance awareness played a crucial role in detecting the suspicious behaviour early. By recognizing the pre-attack indicators and reporting them to security, she helped prevent a security breach.

Lessons Learned:
This scenario illustrates the value of training non-security personnel in hostile reconnaissance awareness. Reception staff, in particular, are often the first point of contact for visitors and can provide an essential layer of security when properly trained.

Debriefing and Reporting Processes

After identifying and disrupting a hostile reconnaissance attempt, a thorough debriefing process is critical. Debriefing allows security personnel to review the incident, evaluate their response, and identify areas for improvement. Key aspects of the debriefing process include:

1. **Detailed Reporting:**
   All security personnel involved in the incident should submit detailed reports outlining their observations, actions taken, and any challenges faced. These reports provide valuable data for future training and risk assessments.
2. **Lessons Learned:**
   The debriefing should focus on what went well and what could be improved. Were there any missed opportunities for earlier detection? Could the situation have been de-escalated more effectively? These insights are essential for refining security procedures.
3. **Updating Protocols:**
   Based on the debriefing, security protocols may need to be updated. This could involve refining the criteria for suspicious behaviour, adjusting staff deployment, or enhancing training programs.

Concluding Thoughts

Hostile reconnaissance is the first step in many criminal and terrorist attacks, making it essential for security personnel to detect and disrupt this activity early. By understanding the stages of hostile reconnaissance and recognizing key indicators, Behaviour Detection Officers (BDOs) and other security personnel can prevent attacks before they happen. Training all staff in hostile reconnaissance awareness further strengthens an organization's security posture and ensures that everyone plays a role in maintaining safety.

This chapter has highlighted the critical importance of vigilance, situational awareness, and proactive engagement in countering hostile reconnaissance. As we move forward, it's crucial to continually refine detection techniques and remain prepared for the evolving nature of threats.

Behaviour detection crisis, an analysis of the world politics and the threats that come with it.

Behavior detection crisis refers to the challenges in identifying and responding to emerging threats in a rapidly changing global political landscape. As nations navigate complex relationships, the interplay of domestic and international factors can lead to instability and conflict.

One significant aspect of this crisis is the rise of authoritarian regimes that exploit technology for surveillance and control, often undermining democratic processes. This trend can create a cycle of repression and resistance, leading to civil unrest and international tensions. The ability to detect changes in state behavior or public sentiment becomes crucial for policymakers, as failing to do so may result in underestimating threats or misjudging allies.

Moreover, the proliferation of misinformation and propaganda exacerbates the crisis. Social media platforms can amplify divisive narratives, influencing public opinion and potentially inciting violence. This manipulation of information complicates the task of assessing real threats and understanding the motives behind state actions or non-state actors.

Internationally, the resurgence of great power competition, particularly between the United States and China, presents another layer of complexity. Each nation employs different strategies for influence, from economic coercion to military posturing. Detecting shifts in these strategies requires a nuanced understanding of global dynamics and the motivations driving each state.

Additionally, non-traditional threats such as climate change and pandemics intersect with political behavior. These issues can exacerbate existing tensions, leading to resource conflicts or migration crises that further challenge global stability. The interconnectedness of these threats necessitates a comprehensive approach to behavior detection, incorporating various fields such as intelligence, social science, and environmental studies.

Overall, the behavior detection crisis in world politics reflects a multifaceted challenge, requiring vigilance and adaptability from both state and non-state actors. Understanding the underlying factors that drive behavior is essential for anticipating and mitigating potential threats in an increasingly volatile global environment.

what threats could you encounter in an NFL or MLB, NBA, MLS , World Cup, Rugby Games etc

, potential threats can include:

1. **Crowd-related incidents:** Fights or riots among fans, which can lead to injuries or chaos.
2. **Terrorism:** The possibility of coordinated attacks targeting large public gatherings, including bomb threats or active shooter situations.
3. **Security breaches:** Unauthorized access to restricted areas, which can pose risks to players and officials.
4. **Player safety:** Injuries from on-field actions or unsafe playing conditions, including equipment failure or poor field conditions.
5. **Weather-related disruptions**: Severe weather events that can lead to evacuations or game cancellations.
6. Protest activities: Demonstrations that may disrupt events or lead to confrontations.
7. **Surveillance and privacy concerns:** Unauthorized recording or monitoring of players and officials, potentially leading to privacy violations.
8. **Health risks:** Outbreaks of illness, such as flu or other contagious diseases, particularly in close-contact sports.
9. **Cybersecurity threats:** Hacking incidents targeting team data, fan information, or event infrastructure.
10. **Financial fraud:** Ticket scalping or counterfeit tickets that can lead to financial losses for fans and organizers.

1. Crowd-related Incidents: Fights or Riots Among Fans

- **Description:** Crowd-related incidents often occur in the heat of competition when fans become overly invested in the outcomes. These incidents can escalate from verbal altercations to full-scale riots, especially during high-stakes games or intense rivalries. The sheer number of people can complicate security responses, and injuries are common among both fans and security personnel.
- **Real-world Examples:** The Heysel Stadium disaster during a European Cup final in 1985 tragically resulted in 39 deaths and numerous injuries due to a riot between rival fans. Similar incidents have occurred across different leagues worldwide.
- **Preventive Measures:** Stadiums now use designated seating for rival fan groups, increased surveillance, and strict security measures to control fan movement. Alcohol restrictions are also often enforced during matches prone to heightened emotions.

2. Terrorism: Threats of Coordinated Attacks

- **Description:** Large sporting events represent high-profile targets for terrorist attacks due to their significant public visibility and large crowds. Attacks can include bomb threats, shootings, or vehicle ramming, posing serious risks to public safety.
- **Real-world Examples:** The 1972 Munich Olympics massacre remains a chilling example where a terrorist group took 11 Israeli athletes hostage, ending tragically. More recently, the Stade de France was targeted during the 2015 Paris attacks.
- **Preventive Measures:** Security protocols now include thorough screening, increased police presence, K9 units trained to detect explosives, and emergency response drills. Many events also establish close coordination with local intelligence agencies to monitor and mitigate potential threats.

3. Security Breaches: Unauthorized Access to Restricted Areas

- **Description:** Breaches into restricted areas can endanger players, officials, and VIPs. These incidents can result from fans attempting to meet their idols or intentional intrusions with malicious intent.
- **Real-world Examples:** In 2019, a fan managed to enter the field during a game between the Browns and Steelers, leading to a disruption. Intrusions like these could have serious consequences, especially if the person entering has harmful intentions.
- **Preventive Measures:** Strict access control is enforced with badge identification, secure entry points, and multiple security checkpoints. Newer technologies, like biometric scanning, are also being employed to ensure only authorized individuals have access to restricted zones.

4. Player Safety: Injuries and Unsafe Conditions

- **Description:** Player safety risks extend beyond routine game injuries to include equipment malfunctions, unsafe field conditions, or security breaches. Ensuring the field and equipment meet safety standards is essential to protecting players from preventable injuries.
- **Real-world Examples:** In the 2021 NFL season, the poor condition of the Allegiant Stadium field led to safety concerns, with players slipping due to inadequate field preparation.
- **Preventive Measures:** Routine checks and maintenance of the field and equipment, as well as implementing regulations to ensure quality, help to protect player safety. Additionally, player-specific security escorts to and from the stadium prevent altercations with fans or protestors.

5. Weather-related Disruptions: Severe Weather Events

- **Description:** Unpredictable weather conditions, such as lightning, storms, or extreme heat, can endanger players, staff, and fans alike. These events often require swift decision-making, including game delays, evacuations, or cancellations.
- **Real-world Examples:** In 2019, the Rugby World Cup in Japan faced severe disruptions due to Typhoon Hagibis, leading to game cancellations. Similarly, NFL games have seen delays due to lightning storms.
- **Preventive Measures:** Many leagues now rely on advanced weather monitoring systems and pre-established protocols to ensure timely communication with fans. Evacuation routes are clearly marked, and stadiums are designed to handle large crowds during unexpected evacuations.

6. Protest Activities: Demonstrations and Potential Disruptions

- **Description:** Sporting events can attract protests due to the platform they offer for visibility. These protests may be peaceful, but they can disrupt the event and escalate if emotions run high.
- **Real-world Examples:** During the 2020 NBA playoffs, players protested racial injustice by refusing to play, highlighting the platform sports can offer for social issues. Fans and activists alike have also gathered outside venues to demonstrate on various social issues.
- **Preventive Measures:** Teams and event organizers often collaborate with local law enforcement to manage protests peacefully. Establishing designated protest zones and clear communication with protesters can mitigate the risk of disruption.

7. Surveillance and Privacy Concerns: Unauthorized Monitoring

- **Description:** Surveillance in sports arenas is common to ensure safety; however, unauthorized surveillance targeting athletes, officials, or VIPs poses privacy risks. This includes unauthorized recordings or data breaches.
- **Real-world Examples:** Paparazzi and rogue fans have been known to bypass security for glimpses of players or team strategies. Notably, in the 2007 "Spygate" scandal, the New England Patriots were caught filming rival teams' hand signals, raising privacy and ethics concerns.
- **Preventive Measures:** Increasing awareness of potential privacy violations and employing rigorous surveillance monitoring technologies help manage unauthorized access. In many arenas, surveillance footage is monitored closely for unusual behavior, and incidents are promptly addressed.

8. Health Risks: Illness Outbreaks Among Players and Fans

- **Description:** Close contact sports and crowded stadiums make infectious diseases a real threat, particularly during outbreaks. Viruses like influenza or norovirus can spread rapidly, impacting players, staff, and attendees.
- **Real-world Examples:** The COVID-19 pandemic resulted in canceled or postponed seasons across major leagues, and protocols were implemented to reduce the risk of transmission.
- **Preventive Measures:** League protocols now include health screenings, regular sanitization, and guidelines for social distancing where possible. Additionally, team staff often work with health officials to implement infection-control measures in venues.

9. Cybersecurity Threats: Data and Infrastructure Security

- **Description:** The digital infrastructure supporting modern sports events, including ticketing, scorekeeping, and broadcasting, is vulnerable to cyber-attacks. Targeted attacks could expose sensitive fan data, interfere with broadcasts, or manipulate outcomes.
- **Real-world Examples:** The Tokyo 2020 Olympics faced cyber-attacks aimed at disrupting live streams, and teams have been targeted for their data on players and strategies.
- **Preventive Measures:** Investment in cybersecurity measures, like firewalls and encrypted communications, is essential for protecting both team data and fan information. Teams and leagues frequently collaborate with cybersecurity firms to safeguard against these potential threats.

10. Financial Fraud: Ticket Scalping and Counterfeit Tickets

- **Description:** Ticket scalping and counterfeit ticketing not only deprive fans of legitimate access but can also result in financial losses for organizers. Scalpers use bots to buy tickets in bulk, and counterfeiters use sophisticated techniques to produce fake tickets.
- **Real-world Examples:** The 2019 Rugby World Cup saw hundreds of fans scammed by counterfeit tickets. Online platforms have also struggled to curb ticket scalping, impacting fans who miss out on fair-priced tickets.
- **Preventive Measures:** Many organizations now employ blockchain technology for ticketing, which makes tickets verifiable and traceable. Partnerships with official ticket vendors and secure resale marketplaces also help to combat ticket fraud and improve fan experiences.

Each topic demonstrates the range of security, safety, and ethical challenges that large sporting events face, alongside evolving measures to prevent or mitigate these risks. Together, these expansions can serve as a comprehensive analysis of the threats and countermeasures surrounding major sports events.

Some of the threats detected in the past

While specific lists of BDO-detected incidents that helped avoid major crises are not publicly available due to confidentiality and security, BDO's risk management and cybersecurity divisions have addressed multiple critical threats in various sectors over the past decade. Examples of incidents where BDO helped mitigate risks include:

1. **Healthcare Cybersecurity**: BDO responded to a ransomware attempt that targeted hospital networks, successfully isolating affected servers to prevent disruption of critical patient data access. The incident highlighted the importance of rapid containment and recovery protocols.

2. **Banking & Finance Sector Breach**: BDO worked on an insider-threat detection project where a high-ranking employee attempted unauthorized transfers. Enhanced monitoring caught the anomaly, averting significant financial losses and regulatory fallout.

3. **Critical Infrastructure**: In a case of aging system vulnerability in public utilities, BDO's assessment led to urgent upgrades to prevent potential power grid disruptions from external cyber threats.

4. **Government System Vulnerability**: A large-scale vulnerability within outdated government servers was identified, with BDO advising on immediate remedial steps, preventing a significant leak of sensitive information related to national security.

5. **Public Event Security for High-Profile Sporting Events**: BDO provided digital forensics and monitoring during events like major league sports games, identifying potential threats from unauthorized drones and online ticket fraud attempts. This real-time intervention safeguarded both attendees and event organizers.

These incidents underscore the breadth of BDO's preventative strategies, which have helped avert major disruptions across finance, healthcare, government, and public events. The efforts cover risk areas from insider threats to outdated infrastructure risks, often through cybersecurity enhancements and rapid response frameworks that highlight BDO's preventative focus in high-stakes environment

Here is a list of firms providing Behavior Detection Officer (BDO) and training services across the UK, USA, Europe, Australia, and Canada, along with some company websites where possible:

United Kingdom

1. **Redline Assured Security** - Offers BDO training focused on threat detection in aviation and other high-security environments. trustredline.co.uk
2. **BPS Ltd** - Provides BDO services and training for large venues and public spaces. bps-ltd.org
3. **Intersec Security** - Known for training in behavior detection and counter-terrorism.
4. **ICTS UK & Ireland** - Specializes in security and BDO deployment at transport hubs. icts.co.uk
5. **G4S UK** - Offers BDO and security personnel training for public spaces. g4s.com

United States

1. **S2 Global** - Focuses on behavior detection training within customs and border protection. s2global.com
2. **TSA (Transportation Security Administration)** - Provides training to BDOs at airports to identify suspicious behaviors.
3. **AvSec Consulting** - Specializes in aviation security, including BDO training.
4. **Behavior Detection and Analysis (BDA) Solutions** - Provides BDO services across multiple sectors.
5. **AS Solution** - Delivers BDO training for executives and VIP events.

Europe

1. **Procheck International** (Netherlands) - Focuses on behavior detection in aviation.
2. **SGS Europe** - Provides comprehensive security and BDO training services. sgs.com
3. **ICTS Europe** - Leading provider of BDOs for airports and transport facilities. ictseurope.com
4. **Securitas Europe** - Offers behavior detection services across high-risk sectors. securitas.com
5. **Teldat GmbH** (Germany) - Focuses on advanced BDO technology and services.

Australia

1. **Unified Security Group** - BDO training for high-risk venues and events. unifiedsecurity.com.au
2. **Certis Security Australia** - Provides BDO solutions for public transport. certisgroup.com
3. **Australian Federal Police (AFP)** - Offers specialized behavior detection training for law enforcement.
4. **Wilson Security** - Behavior detection services for commercial and public venues. wilsonsecurity.com.au
5. **MSS Security** - Known for BDO training and security services in high-traffic locations. msssecurity.com.au

Canada

1. **GardaWorld** - Provides behavior detection services across Canada. gardaworld.com
2. **Paladin Security** - Offers BDO and risk management services. paladinsecurity.com
3. **Commissionaires Canada** - Delivers training in behavior detection and security. commissionaires.ca
4. **Securitas Canada** - Known for deploying BDOs in large public spaces. securitas.ca
5. **Avigilon** - Focuses on behavior analytics technology and security solutions. avigilon.com

These firms provide critical training and deployment of Behavior Detection Officers, primarily in high-risk, high-footfall areas such as airports, transport hubs, and large events.

Here are examples of Behavior Detection Officer (BDO) training and service firms across Africa, Mexico, Latin America, Asia, and the Middle East. These firms provide essential security services, including threat assessment, behavioral analysis, and surveillance, often working with large public events, transportation sectors, and governmental agencies:

Africa

1. **Baseline Plus** – United Kingdom-based with training in Africa, specializing in threat detection and behavioral analysis for high-security environments. baseline-plus.com
2. **MAGENTA Consulting** – Operates in Africa and offers behavioral insights and security training. magentaconsulting.org
3. **HAE Group (TSA Group)** – Provides behavioral detection training for aviation and large-scale events, including threat management and compliance programs in Africa. tsagp.com
4. **Control Risks Group** – Specializes in risk management and provides training for BDO roles across Africa. controlrisks.com

Mexico and Latin America

1. **Secure Solutions Mexico** – Offers behavioral and threat detection training specifically tailored for public venues and transportation. securesolutionsmexico.com
2. **AS3 International** – Based in Mexico with a Latin America focus, providing specialized training in behavior detection for corporate clients. as3international.com
3. **Prosegur** – A leading security company across Latin America offering behavioral training and monitoring solutions. prosegur.com
4. **Grupo SIPRO** – Located in Latin America, SIPRO specializes in customized security services, including behavior analysis for events and public spaces. gruposipro.com

Asia

1. **TSA Group** – Provides specialized BDO and behavioral training in compliance with international standards, working widely across Asia. tsagp.com
2. **Kroll** – Global risk consulting firm offering behavior detection and security consulting in Asia. kroll.com
3. **G4S Asia** – Operates extensively in Asia, offering behavioral analysis and on-the-ground threat detection services. g4s.com
4. **Secom** – Japan-based, Secom provides high-level security services, including behavioral detection, across several Asian countries. secom.co.jp

Middle East (Arabia)

1. **Rapiscan Systems** – Provides security technology and behavior detection training across the Middle East, with a focus on high-security environments. rapiscansystems.com
2. **MAGENTA Consulting** – Operates throughout the Middle East offering customized behavior detection training and consulting services. magentaconsulting.org
3. **ICTS Middle East** – Specializes in behavior detection for aviation and public events. icts.co.uk
4. **SGS** – Offers a variety of security services, including behavior detection and training programs across the Middle East. sgs.com

These firms provide varying levels of training and threat detection services, ensuring enhanced security through behavioral analysis, risk assessment, and on-site management for public gatherings, airports, and corporate clients. They work closely with international security standards and bring regional knowledge tailored to the risks present in each area.

Here's a list of 20 behavior detection and security training companies in Israel that specialize in counterterrorism, security strategy, and threat detection, offering advanced training services both nationally and internationally:

1. **Aaron Cohen Tactical Training**
   aaroncohensecurity.com
   Provides high-stakes counterterrorism and behavioral detection training for military and law enforcement.

2. **ISA Academy**
   isaacademy.com
   Focuses on behavioral detection and counter-terror training for public and private sector security teams.

3. **Magal Security Systems**
   magalsecurity.com
   Known for perimeter security and integrated behavioral analysis systems in critical infrastructure protection.

4. **Athena Security**
   athenasecurity.com
   Specializes in AI-powered threat detection and behavioral monitoring solutions.

5. **Elbit Systems Security Training**
   elbitsystems.com
   Provides advanced surveillance and situational awareness training integrated with defense technology.

6. **IMI Systems Security Training**

imi-israel.com

Offers specialized training programs in behavior analysis for security professionals and government agencies.

7. **Shaldag Security**

shaldag.com

Delivers behavioral threat detection training, specializing in counterterrorism and high-security consulting.

8. **Krav Maga Israel Defense**

kravmaga.co.il

Combines self-defense with behavioral threat assessment and rapid response training.

9. **Counter-Terror & Security Solutions**

ctssecurity.com

Provides counter-terrorism and detection training focusing on body language and behavioral anomalies.

10. **Israel Tactical School**

israeltacticalschool.com

Focuses on elite counter-terrorism tactics, including behavioral detection and rapid response.

11. **Protective Edge Security Solutions**

protectiveedgesecurity.com

Trains security personnel in advanced behavioral profiling techniques for critical situations.

12. **SecurePlus Israel**

secureplus.com

Offers customized behavioral detection and risk management training for businesses and security agencies.

13. **Protex**

protex.co.il

Provides security consulting and training with a strong focus on behavioral threat detection.

14. Ben Gurion University - Homeland Security Studies

bgu.ac.il

Offers specialized courses in behavioral detection within homeland security contexts.

15. **TAR Ideal Concepts**

tarideal.com

A security company providing behavioral threat assessment training alongside tactical response programs.

16. **ZAKA Emergency Response**

zaka.org.il

Known for handling critical incidents, offering training in behavioral detection for rapid emergency response.

17. **Security Israel Academy**

securityisrael.co.il

Provides training courses on security assessments, including crowd behavior analysis.

18. **IBEX Solutions**

ibexsolutions.com

Specializes in training focused on behavior-based threat detection and intelligence solutions.

19. **Moked Services**

moked911.co.il

Offers a range of security training including behavioral detection and real-time surveillance.

20. **Homeland Security Experts Israel**

homelandsecurityexperts.com

Provides consultancy and training in behavioral threat detection, focusing on security preparedness.